Come With Me, Together We'll See the Beauty of...

HAWAII

By Jeannie & Madison Fung
Illustrated by Patty Nunn Iba

We hope you enjoy our book!
aloha!
Jeannie Fung
Madison Fung

This book is dedicated to

Daddy

Thank you for working so hard for us so that we can spend
time together on these wonderful vacations. We love you and
can't wait for our next trip together real soon.

JSM

Published by CreateSpace
First Edition
ISBN 978-0-578-18737-2
www.thefungroupbooks.com
Manufactured in the U.S.A.

Where **ALOHA** means hello and goodbye

And **PALM TREES** grow as high as the sky.

Where the **HIBISCUS** is the official state flower

And a **RAINBOW** appears after a light shower.

Where fresh **ORCHIDS** and **PLUMERIAS**

are strung into a beautiful **LEI**

And golden **SUNSETS** can be seen almost everyday.

Where there are hundreds of beautiful **BEACHES** to explore

With fluffy **SAND** and unique **SEASHELLS** along the shore.

Where **SURFING** and **SNORKELING**

are favorite things to do,

Even **KAYAKING** and **CANOEING**

are just as fun too!

Where the **HUMU HUMU NUKU NUKU APU A'A**

is the official state fish.

It's also the longest Hawaiian word there is,

so try catching it, you can only wish.

Where a traditional **LUAU** feast is part of the Island's history

And girls put on **GRASS SKIRTS** to dance the **HULA** for all to see.

Where little kids are called **KEIKIS.**

They have fun dancing and singing

to the sounds of **UKULELES.**

Where ladies dress in their favorite traditional **MUUMUUS**,

Even the grandparents...they call them **TUTUS**.

Where **PINEAPPLES** and **PAPAYAS** are juicy and sweet

And **SHAVE ICE** is a cool refreshing treat.

Where you can use your fingers to eat a dish called **POI**

Made out of **TARO**...it's healthy so enjoy!

Where **PEARL HARBOR** is memorialized

For all those people who lost their lives.

Where there's still an active **VOLCANO**

Near where **KONA COFFEE**

and **SUGARCANE** grow.

Where there are hundreds of fancy

HOTELS & RESORTS to stay

That offer swimming **POOLS, GOLF,**

SPA, and **TENNIS** to play.

Where you can hike up to majestic WATERFALLS

Past GARDENS filled with TROPICAL PLANTS

that are lush and tall.

Once ruled by **KING KAMEHAMEHA** and family
more than 200 years ago to date,
HAWAII is now our **50TH STATE.**

KAUAI

OAHU

MOLOKAI

LANAI

MAUI

BIG ISLAND
OF HAWAII

Let's visit **OAHU**, the **BIG ISLAND, MAUI & KAUAI**

And don't forget there's also **LANAI & MOLOKAI!**

On these Islands, there's so much to see and do.

We've only mentioned just a few.

But what makes **HAWAII** so special to see?

It's **OHANA** – being able to share it all with my family!

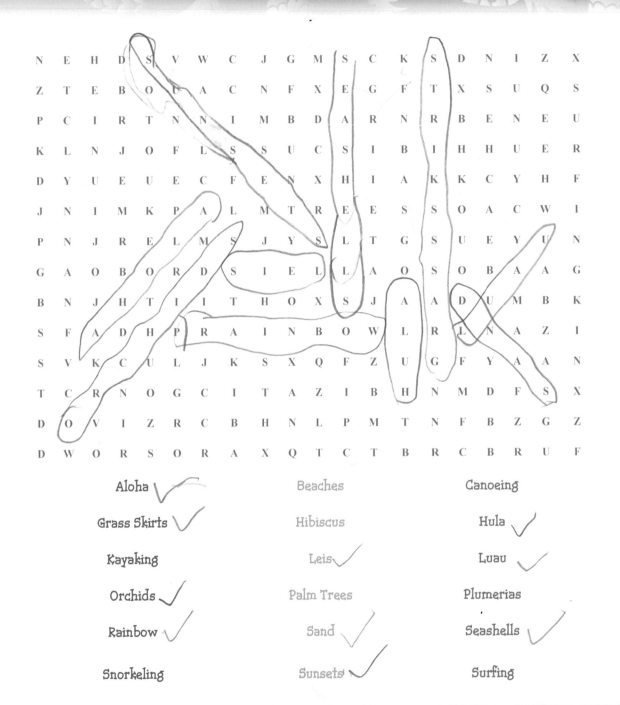

N	E	H	D	S	V	W	C	J	G	M	S	C	K	S	D	N	I	Z	X
Z	T	E	B	O	U	A	C	N	F	X	E	G	F	T	X	S	U	Q	S
P	C	I	R	T	N	I	M	B	D	A	R	N	R	B	E	N	E	U	U
K	L	N	J	O	F	L	S	S	U	C	S	I	B	I	H	H	U	E	R
D	Y	U	E	U	E	C	F	E	N	X	H	I	A	K	K	C	Y	H	F
J	N	I	M	K	P	A	L	M	T	R	E	E	S	S	O	A	C	W	I
P	N	J	R	E	L	M	S	J	Y	S	L	T	G	S	U	E	Y	U	N
G	A	O	B	O	R	D	S	I	E	L	L	A	O	S	O	B	A	A	G
B	N	J	H	T	I	I	T	H	O	X	S	J	A	A	D	U	M	B	K
S	F	A	D	H	P	R	A	I	N	B	O	W	L	R	L	N	A	Z	I
S	V	K	C	U	L	J	K	S	X	Q	F	Z	U	G	F	Y	A	A	N
T	C	R	N	O	G	C	I	T	A	Z	I	B	H	N	M	D	F	S	X
D	O	V	I	Z	R	C	B	H	N	L	P	M	T	N	F	B	Z	G	Z
D	W	O	R	S	O	R	A	X	Q	T	C	T	B	R	C	B	R	U	F

Aloha ✓	Beaches	Canoeing
Grass Skirts ✓	Hibiscus	Hula ✓
Kayaking	Leis ✓	Luau ✓
Orchids ✓	Palm Trees	Plumerias
Rainbow ✓	Sand ✓	Seashells ✓
Snorkeling	Sunsets ✓	Surfing

ACROSS
3. Traditional Hawaiian feast
4. Hello or goodbye
7. Appears after a light shower
10. Where you can find sand and seashells
12. A tropical fruit
13. Flower necklaces
15. Grandparents
16. A sport that uses clubs, balls and tees

DOWN
1. Hawaiian dance
2. A mountain that can erupt
5. Family
6. A cool refreshing treat
8. A beautiful river runoff
9. Little kids
11. Official state flower
14. A popular water sport

Unscramble the Following Words:

1. erlPa rbHaor   _____ _____
2. caoVoln   _____
3. uMusuum   _____
4. iKseik   _____
5. uuaL   _____
6. uTusl   _____
7. oraT   _____
8. Sahve ecl   _____ ____
9. leklsUeu   _____
10. Pyaapa   _____
11. peleniapP   _____
12. oPi   ____
13. augSr neac   _____ _____
14. oKan Ceeoff eaBns   _____ _____ _____

How Many Words Can You Make Out Of:

HUMUHUMUNUKUNUKUAPUA'A and KING KAMEHAMEHA

1	11
2	12
3	13
4	14
5	15
6	16
7	17
8	18
9	19
10	20

```
T  S  U  A  O  I  H  X  N  Y  S  I  G  A  J  V  E  D  I  S
R  F  R  A  H  O  Q  K  S  L  S  I  O  B  P  K  T  X  T  L
F  E  H  Y  T  E  P  N  L  D  N  A  L  E  P  S  A  J  K  C
M  U  S  E  X  J  M  A  E  Q  Y  W  F  M  V  B  T  L  D  P
X  T  L  O  T  J  F  A  F  D  H  A  Y  O  P  J  S  L  W  X
K  S  T  H  R  R  C  O  H  R  R  H  N  L  L  N  H  A  X  E
S  I  N  N  E  T  I  Q  H  E  X  A  B  O  L  T  T  Z  P  T
I  W  F  T  G  A  S  D  D  A  M  U  G  K  R  T  E  P  K  Y
S  V  A  A  U  R  E  V  L  A  N  A  I  A  Z  B  I  O  G  B
B  W  B  A  M  Q  V  I  E  G  G  A  K  I  T  D  T  B  X  P
F  C  K  G  T  R  F  U  M  N  S  B  L  G  O  A  F  F  D  E
S  T  N  A  L  P  L  A  C  I  P  O  R  T  N  M  I  J  K  P
B  I  G  I  S  L  A  N  D  T  V  G  Q  G  W  I  F  Y  F  Q
I  U  A  M  O  L  M  C  W  S  A  G  E  X  O  T  K  T  D  K
```

Big Island	Fiftieth State	Garden
Golf	Hawaii	Hotels
Kauai	King Kamehameha	Lanai
Maui	Molokai	Oahu
Ohana	Resorts	Spa
Tennis	Tropical Plants	Waterfalls

44860629R00018

Made in the USA
San Bernardino, CA
25 January 2017